REAL EYES
REALIZE

Any unauthorized use of the content, including but not limited to:

- Copying or reproducing text in whole or in part
- Downloading or disseminating the book in electronic form
- Using excerpts or images from the book for any purpose, including educational, commercial, or promotional use

is a violation of copyright law and may subject the infringing party to legal action.

4. Fair Use Doctrine

While the Author respects the principles of fair use, any use that exceeds the bounds of fair use must be approached with caution. Educational institutions and individuals wishing to use portions of the text for scholarly purposes should seek permission. Fair use is assessed on a case-by-case basis and generally considers factors such as:

- The purpose and character of the use (commercial vs. educational)
- The nature of the copyrighted work
- The amount and substantiality of the portion used about the whole work
- The effect of the use upon the market for the original work

5. Enforcement of Rights

The Author is committed to enforcing their rights under copyright law. Any individual or organization found to violate these rights will be subject to legal action, including but not limited to the following:

- Cease and desist orders
- Monetary damages

- Injunctive relief to prevent further unauthorized use

6. Contact Information for Permissions

For inquiries regarding permissions, licensing agreements, or any questions about this legal notice, please contact:

Kaashif Shahul Hameed
The address and Mail of the author are not disclosed upon the author's request.
@kaashifshahulhameed

7. Conclusion

We appreciate your cooperation in respecting these rights and adhering to copyright laws. The Author wishes to thank the readers for their support and interest in this literary work.

Respectfully,

Kaachu

Preface

As you embark on the journey through the pages of this book, I want to take a moment to address something of utmost importance. This message serves as a gentle reminder and a thoughtful clarification regarding the content you are about to explore. I need to convey that the stories and themes presented in this book are products of imagination and creativity and are not intended to cause harm, discomfort, or distress to anyone.

This book delves into a variety of subjects and narratives that are designed to entertain, provoke thought, and offer a unique perspective on various issues. The scenarios, characters, and events depicted within these pages are fictional or dramatized for storytelling. They are created to engage readers and stimulate emotional and intellectual responses, but they are not meant to reflect real-life situations or to target, offend, or distress any individual or group.

The creative process behind this book involves exploring complex themes and emotions, often through exaggerated or fantastical elements. This approach is intended to provide a compelling reading experience, encouraging readers to reflect on different aspects of life, society, and human nature. While the content may touch on serious or sensitive topics, please remember that these are presented within the context of fiction and artistic expression.

It is important to understand that the stories in this book are crafted with the utmost respect and sensitivity towards all individuals and communities. The intent is never to belittle, harm, or cause any form of emotional discomfort. If any part of the book feels troubling or uncomfortable, I encourage you to approach it with the knowledge that it is a work of fiction, created to explore themes in a controlled and imaginative setting.

The narratives within this book may sometimes tackle challenging or controversial subjects. This approach is intended to provoke thought and spark conversations, not to cause harm or perpetuate negative stereotypes. Fiction has the power to explore a wide range of human experiences and perspectives, and this book aims to do so in a manner that is respectful and considerate. If you find yourself affected by any content, please remember that it is important to prioritize your well-being. Taking breaks, discussing your feelings with trusted friends or family, or seeking professional support are all valid steps if needed.

Your emotional and mental well-being is of paramount importance. Literature, while a powerful tool for reflection and growth, should never come at the expense of your comfort or safety. As a writer and storyteller, I aim to create a space where readers can engage with thought-provoking content while feeling secure in the understanding that the work is meant to be a form of artistic expression.

If you encounter any themes or elements in the book that you find particularly distressing or challenging, please remember that you have the agency to pause, reflect, or step away as needed. It is perfectly okay to engage with content at your own pace and in a manner that feels right for you. Your boundaries and comfort are important, and respecting them is crucial for a positive reading experience.

Furthermore, this book is intended to be a source of enjoyment and enrichment and not to serve as a trigger or source of unnecessary discomfort. The intention behind every story, character, and plot twist is to provide a meaningful and engaging narrative rather than to cause harm or provoke negative reactions.

The creative choices made are guided by a desire to offer a thoughtful and immersive experience, and I deeply hope that this intention is clear throughout the book.

As readers, your engagement with the content is invaluable, and your ability to approach it with an open mind while maintaining personal boundaries is greatly appreciated. Literature has the power to challenge, inspire, and connect us, and it is my sincere hope that this book contributes positively to your reading experience.

In summary, I want to reiterate that the stories and themes within this book are meant to be explored as works of fiction and creativity. They are crafted to entertain and provoke thought, but never to harm or distress. Your comfort and well-being are important, and if you find any content challenging, please remember that you can engage with it at your own pace and seek support if needed.

Thank you for taking the time to read this book and for being a valued part of this creative journey. Your support and engagement are deeply appreciated, and I hope that the stories within bring you enjoyment, reflection, and inspiration.

Dear Readers,

As I sit down to write this, I am overwhelmed with a profound sense of gratitude and reflection. It's both humbling and exhilarating to think about the incredible journey we've undertaken together, and I want to take this moment to express my heartfelt thanks to every one of you. Your unwavering support, enthusiasm, and engagement have been the cornerstone of this endeavor, and I am deeply appreciative of the role you've played in making our shared experience so meaningful and successful.

When I first embarked on this project, it was driven by a vision— a vision to create a space where stories could not only entertain but also inspire, connect, and uplift. I imagined a community where readers and creators could come together, sharing ideas, emotions, and experiences through the power of storytelling. It was a dream fuelled by a love for the written word and a belief in its ability to forge connections and spark imaginations. The journey from that initial spark to the thriving community we have now has been nothing short of extraordinary, and it's all thanks to you.

From the very beginning, your support has been instrumental in bringing this vision to life. Every comment, every share, and every moment of engagement has contributed to shaping the direction and success of our work. Knowing that our stories have found a place in your lives, that they've resonated with you in some way, is the highest reward we could hope for. Your feedback, whether through kind words, constructive criticism, or enthusiastic endorsements, has been invaluable in guiding and refining our content. It's your reactions and insights that help us understand what works, what resonates, and how we can continue to grow and improve.

One of the most rewarding aspects of this journey has been watching our community evolve. It's amazing how storytelling has the power to unite people from all walks of life, creating a shared space where diverse voices and perspectives come together. Our community has become more than just a collection of readers; it's a vibrant, interconnected group of individuals who share a passion for stories and a curiosity about the world. Your contributions—whether through thoughtful discussions, sharing personal reflections, or participating in our various activities—have fostered a dynamic and supportive environment where creativity and dialogue thrive.

I am continually moved by the impact our work has had on you. It's incredibly fulfilling to hear how a particular story or article has provided comfort, inspiration, or a moment of escape. Your personal stories and feedback remind me why this work is so important. Each piece we create is crafted with the hope of touching lives, sparking new ideas, or simply offering a moment of enjoyment. Knowing that our efforts have made a difference, that they've had a positive impact on your lives, is a testament to the power of storytelling and the strength of our community.

The support and encouragement you've shown have been especially meaningful during challenging times. Every creative endeavour faces its share of obstacles and setbacks, and there have been moments when doubt and difficulty seemed overwhelming. However, your unwavering belief in our work and your encouraging words have been a source of strength and motivation. Your presence, whether through a kind comment or a word of encouragement, reinforces the value of our efforts and helps us persevere through the tough times.

As we look to the future, I am filled with excitement and anticipation. We have many plans and ideas for the coming months, and we're eager to continue exploring new themes, expanding our horizons, and delivering content that meets your interests and passions. Your ongoing support will be crucial as we navigate this path and strive to bring you stories and experiences that resonate deeply. We are committed to evolving and growing, and your continued engagement will play a key role in shaping the direction we take.

In a rapidly changing world, it's easy to overlook the impact of seemingly small but significant moments. But I want you to know that every interaction you have with our work is deeply valued. Your presence here, whether you've been with us from the start or have joined us recently, is an integral part of our journey. The connection we share through storytelling is a testament to the power of words and the strength of our community. Each of you contributes to the richness of this experience, and for that, I am profoundly grateful.

I also want to acknowledge the hard work and dedication of everyone involved in bringing our content to you. Behind the scenes, many individuals contribute their talents, time, and energy to ensure that we deliver the best possible work. Their commitment and passion are reflected in every piece of content we share, and I am incredibly thankful for their contributions. Together, we strive to create something that not only meets your expectations but also inspires and uplifts.

As we continue this journey together, I want to express my deepest appreciation for your support. It's an honour to have you as part of this community, and I am excited about the future and the many stories we will share. Your engagement, feedback, and enthusiasm are the driving forces behind our work, and they make every challenge and triumph worthwhile. Thank you for believing in our vision, for participating in our shared experience, and for making this journey so rewarding.

In closing, I want to extend my heartfelt thanks once again. Your support means more to me than words can fully express, and I am deeply grateful for every one of you. Here's to continuing this adventure together, exploring new stories, and creating even more memorable moments. Your presence and participation are the heart and soul of this endeavour, and I look forward to many more chapters and experiences with you.

With deepest appreciation and warmest regards,

Kaachu

~This is a collection of all randomness that I've felt over and over in my head~

Him

In the quiet dawn when shadows start to wane,
He rises early, bearing life's refrain,
A steady hand, a heart both strong and kind,
In every line of his, pure love you'll find.

His laughter is a beacon in the night,
A guiding star that shines with endless light,
Through trials faced and moments dark and cold,
His wisdom warms a story yet untold.

With calloused hands and patience deep and true,
He teaches lessons both in words and deeds,
In every challenge faced, he sees us through,
And plants in us the strength to chase our needs.

He's more than just a figure tall and grand,
He's tender whispers and a gentle hand,
A fortress in the storms that life may send,
A steadfast rock, a guide, a faithful friend.

In memories of walks and talks we share,
Of bedtime tales and dreams beyond compare,
He's woven in the fabric of our days,
A legacy of love in countless ways.

So, to Dad, whose heart forever beats,
In every triumph and each defeat,
A hero not in capes, but in his grace,
A timeless love no time can e'er erase.

1/1

Her

In the hush of morning's tender light,
You are the warmth that chases out the night,
With every touch, a solace soft and pure,
Your love is constant, steadfast, and secure.

You are the heart where endless patience grows,
A gentle guide through all life's highs and lows,
In every smile, a thousand words unspoken,
In every hug, a promise never broken.

Your hands have crafted more than just a home,
They've built a world where love and kindness roam,
In every meal, in every quiet song,
A testament to where our hearts belong.

Through sleepless nights that stretch and bend,
You've been the anchor, the family's closest friend,
A lighthouse shining brightly through the storm,
A heart of gold that keeps us safe and warm.

In every lesson taught with tender care,
In every story shared, a truth laid bare,
You've shown us how to love with all we are,
A guiding light, our brightest, fiercest star.

Dear Mom, with endless grace,
With love and gratitude that time can't erase,
For all the dreams you've nurtured and the ways,
You've filled our lives with light through all the days.
2/2

Forever

One's heart might be bound by ribs,

It might be caged, but not its beat.

One's brain might be enclosed in a skull,

Not his memory.

A man might die,

Not his ideas.

3/3

I've always wondered why the heart is bound by ribs and the brain by the skull, have you?

Hierarchy

Red, a colour of hierarchy,

Life;

The senescence of wild rose,

Death;

Redness pumped up your vein,

Till the last breath,

A black man's blood ain't black,

A fair man's blood ain't white,

Then why is this thought out of sight?

4/4

Canvas

Chest's a canvas,

If you develop closeness,

Letting people paint is art,

Remember, it is meddling with your heart.

Scars do heal,

Not what we feel.

5/5

.

Time aims to kill me, so don't I have the right to kill some of it?

Think about it; it makes sense, doesn't it?

5/5

Disagreed

People age like fine wine, said a monk,

Better and finer every day,

I disagreed,

I said,

Once young and gay,

Now frail and dead.

6/6

I've seen a 50-year-old man and a 15-year-old man read this line again.

I refuse

I'd rather die in a dream than live in it,

Don't wish for a well-lit life,

Don't ignore it,

Or say so be it.

7/7

Her and I

The sky weeps with us,

Blue and black; the thunder clap,

Pouring down the sky,

Tears down our eyes.

You and I apart,

Like the moon and stars at war.

8/8

Told to

Told to have some etiquette, isn't it?

Told how to and not to,

Coordinated by a system of shit,

The ones who escape it are people with some wit.

The one who introduced such ridicule might be dead,

If you couldn't move the way you want in chess,

Then you're a pawn with no sword.

9/9

Would you sew it back?

I'd lend you a needle,

To sew my torn heart,

Promise me,

That you wouldn't use it,

To tear my heart again.

10/10

Never let someone do the deed twice.

Poet

Blood spilled,

Tears served,

It is harder said than done,

Every time, his words won.

11/11

We cry and bleed on pages.

Hurt

Eyelids close like curtains,

Hide hurt.

Lips zipped shut,

Restrain a spectrum of emotions.

12/12

**Most people would choose to shed blood rather than tears.
Sometimes holding a rose could prick you badly even if it
you call it love.**

In a box

Cigarettes don't hurt as long as you don't light them,
So does your heart,
The sky isn't the limit as long as you think beyond,
So does your mind,
Might be grown in a box called home,
So does your heart and brain by bones.
Caught and kept,
Because the more you grow, the wilder it gets.

13/13

Grey

Shades of grey and navy,
Darkness engulfing my light,
Partially blinded even with my eyes wide open,
That is all that I could see.

I ain't blind,
But told to act as if I am.

Still living but feel dead,
All those I loved,
Ain't dead and lost,
But living with a dead heart.

Took the best of my heart,
And left the rest in pieces.
I stitched it again,
But it still fell apart.

I do have a heart,
Heavy and wounded,
Beating for a dead man,
To remind him that he's still living.

Most people die young,
But are buried late.

What's the point of it beating?
When I am already dead.
14/14

Ache
Used to suffer, long ago,
Now, I have adopted pain as my friend,
As it might be the only one to never leave me.

Shadows don't disappear,
But no one questions its existence,
Nor its use,
So does pain.

15/15

Deep cuts

In the labyrinth of shadows cast,
Where echoes of the past are lost,
The heartache lingers, deep and vast,
A heavy cost for dreams long tossed.

To be lost is to wander blind,
Through corridors of a fractured mind,
Each step a whisper of despair,
A silent cry in the midnight air.

The wounds of hurt, they bleed and sting,
A cruel reminder of forgotten spring,
Where joy once bloomed, now turned to grey,
And hope seems but a fleeting day.

16/16

Lost feelings

Once had feelings
Runs in my veins, dark and lush,
Deprived and dry, still it flows,
Lost its nature, tamed by other,
Offended by its audacity.
It's what I desire, it's what it is,
It's the blood that keeps me high.
Warm it was, in my young tender heart,
Now cold and hard, inside a chamber of a living man.

17/7

Time flows

In the quiet hush of dawn's embrace,
Time flows like a river, slow and grand,
Carrying whispers of a distant place,
And dreams that slip through our open hands.

Moments drift by like leaves on a stream,
Glimmering fragments of what used to be,
Still and serene, like a half-forgotten dream,
Yet rushing forward, wild and free.

The river of time bends and sways,
Eroding cliffs of yesterday's might,
Washing away the shadows of olden days,
Merging with the vastness of endless night.

Each drop a memory, clear and bright,
Reflecting the sun of our shared past,
Yet slipping away with the fading light,
In a current too swift to hold fast.

Still, we dip our hands in its flow,
Grasping at moments we cannot keep,
Finding solace in the ebb and flow,
In the river's song, both gentle and deep.

So let it carry us, wherever it leads,
Through the calm pools and tempest's roar,
For in its depths, our heart finds what it needs,
The echoes of time, forevermore.

Cut it off

Hurts a lot, still it stayed,

Slayed it off, isn't it the only way?

Had a couple of them over these years,

If life is a thing, isn't it meant for wear and tear?

19/19

Try and deny

Roses are red,

Violets are blue,

Our first meeting wasn't the day when I fell for you.

All roses are not red,

All violets are not blue,

I cannot deny my feelings for you.

20/20

Lies wrapped in silk

Bound by veins,

Thought they were humans,

Still, it's a lie wrapped in silk,

I've been told too many lies, I melted, I folded, I creased,

I believed too much, I bled,

Did I just let my heart burn?

21/21

Lost in you

Beneath a sky of twilight's tender hue,
Where stars like scattered whispers gently gleam,
I find my heart entwined and lost in you,
As if our love were written in a dream.

The moonlight bathes your eyes in silver grace,
A dance of shadows on your gentle skin,
And in the silence of this sacred space,
I hear the symphony of where we've been.

Your touch, a brush of warmth upon my soul,
A promise woven in the threads of night,
Together, we are fragments made whole,
Our hearts alight with love's eternal light.

In every breath, a melody of care,
In every glance, a story left untold,
With you, my love, I have found my air,
A tale of passion that will never fold.

So let the world outside our bubble spin,
For in your arms, I've found my place, my home,
With every sunrise, let our journey begin,
Forever bound, together, we will roam.

22/22

Why wait?

To live is not to sit in idle grace,
Nor wait for time to draw its fleeting line,
But to embrace the world with an open face,
And dance within each moment, pure and fine.

To live is to ignite the morning sun,
With passions bright that spark from deep within,
To greet each day as though a race begun,
Where every breath and heartbeat is a win.

To live is not in dreams alone confined,
But in the steps we take with courage bold,
In laughter shared, and in the hearts entwined,
In stories told, and every hand we hold.

To live is to be present in the now,
To find the wonder in the smallest things,
To face the storm and feel the gentle vow,
Of love that through the fleeting tempest sings.

To live is to embrace the highs and lows,
To cherish moments both of joy and pain,
To grow with every seed of life that sows,
And dance beneath the sun, despite the rain.

So let us live as verbs, not passive still,
To shape our fate with every choice we make,
And in the rhythm of each dream fulfilled,
To find the essence of the life we take.

23/23

One and only friend

In a world so vast and shadowed by the tide,
Where countless faces drift and paths divide,
I stumbled on a soul, a light so rare,
A beacon in the dark, beyond compare.

Through fleeting moments and the endless chase,
In crowded rooms, your presence was my space,
You understood the silence in my eyes,
A friend who saw through masks and thin disguise.

When words felt lost and dreams seemed out of reach,
You offered solace and taught me how to teach.
My heart to trust, to find a gentle way,
To navigate the storm and find the day.

In laughter shared and tears that freely flowed,
You walked beside me on the roads I strode,
Your kindness, like a compass, pointed true,
In every trial faced, I found in you.

Though friends may come and go like shifting sands,
Your steadfast spirit was a touch of hands,
A promise made, a bond that time refines,
In you, a friendship that forever shines.

So, here's to you, the only friend I've known,
In every memory and every tone,
For in the heart of one, I found my place,
A treasured gift, a rare and loving grace.

24/24

Society's rules are just whispers of conformity; true freedom lies in the courage to question and **defy** them.

25/25

Trading this life

If I could trade this life for dreams untold,
Where aspirations gleam in hues of gold,
I'd barter all the hours and moments spent,
For a vision where my heart is truly bent.

In dreams, the sky is vast, a canvas free,
A realm where every wish can truly be,
Where limits fade and possibilities expand,
And I can grasp the stars with trembling hand.

To trade this life for dreams would mean release,
From every doubt and every whispered cease,
To dive into the boundless, bright unknown,
And find the place where all my hopes have grown.

Yet in this life, though dreams are not yet grasped,
I cherish moments where the present are clasped,
For dreams are threads we weave with courage bold,
And life itself, a story yet to be told.

So, though the trade is tempting, sweet, and grand,
I'll cherish both the dreams and what I've planned,
For in this life, the dream is mine to chase,
And every breath I take is filled with grace.

26/26

You hurt me

In the expanse of day and endless blue,
The sky reflects a girl's wide, hopeful view,
Both open realms where dreams and visions play,
Both are vast and boundless in their display.

The sky, a canvas brushed with hues so bright,
Holds sunlight's warmth and shadows of the night,
Its changing face from dawn to twilight's hue,
Mirrors the girl's shifts from old to new.

The girl, a world of wonder yet untamed,
With laughter's light and sorrows unashamed,
Her eyes like stars that pierce the twilight's veil,
In every glance, a universe is unveiled.

Yet in the heart where deepest feelings start,
A tender space where joy and pain depart,
The heart beats strong but often bears the sting,
Of hurt that time and love together bring.

The hurt, a shadow on the heart's pure grace,
A mark of trials faced, a shitty trace,
Yet like the sky's own stormy, fleeting gales,
It passes, leaving hope where light prevails.

The girl and sky, both reflect and bend,
As heart and hurt, through time, both mend and blend,
For in their dance of joy and aching rue,
They find the strength to start anew.

27/27

The Painter and the eyes

A painter stands before a white canvas white,
With colours mixed to capture deepest night,
Yet in his heart, a sorrow softly lies,
Reflected in the shades of someone's eyes.

His brush, a wand that dances with the pain,
Finds echoes of the hurt in every stain,
He paints the shadows of a love once bright,
Now dimmed and lost within the fading light.

Those eyes, like pools of melancholy deep,
Hold stories that the silent heart will keep,
A sea of hurt where gentle waves collide,
With dreams that drift and hopes that now subside.

He daubs the canvas with a wistful hue,
Of blues and greys, where tears have once been true,
Each stroke a testament to feelings worn,
Of moments shared, now fractured and forlorn.

In every line and every subtle shade,
The painter weaves the sorrow love has made,
He captures not just beauty, but the ache,
Of eyes that hold the hurt of hearts that break.

Yet in this art, there's solace, strange and pure,
For through the hurt, the painter's touch endures,
He finds in every painful, heartfelt guise,
A portrait of the love within those eyes.

As colours blend and shadows gently fall,
The painter captures echoes of a call,
A plea for healing in the strokes of grace,
A reflection of the love time can't erase.

With every hue, he mends the heart's deep seam,
Transforming sorrow into soft, bright dreams,
His brush becomes a balm for wounds unseen,
An artful touch on canvases serene.

The eyes that hold the pain are now alive,
In every stroke, they find a way to thrive,
A testament to love that remains,
Despite the hurt, through beauty, it refrains.

In every portrait, in each tender line,
He weaves the story of a heart divine,
A journey from the depths of aching night,
To dawn's embrace and love's enduring light.

The painter steps back, gazing at his work,
A masterpiece of hope where shadows lurk,
For through the hurt and pain, a truth is known—
That love, though tested, can always be shown.

So, as he views the eyes, he's painted clear,
He finds a solace in the art he's near,
In every brushstroke, every heartfelt shade,
The pain of love, in beauty, is remade.

28/28

Rebellion's echo

In the cacophony of societal chants,
Where conformity's grip holds firm and tight,
I shout into the void where silence plants,
A call to break from the shadows of the night.

"Shit society," I cry with fervent breath,
For in its mould, my spirit cannot thrive,
Its rules and norms, like chains of weary death,
Suppress the fire that helps the soul survive.

Its whispers try to dim the brightest flame,
To mould us into figures dull and grey,
But I refuse to bear this stifling shame,
And, walk instead a path that leads away.

From labels sewn and judgments harshly cast,
I turn my back and forge a different way,
For in the heart of rebellion, vast,
Lies freedom's breath and truth's unyielding sway.

So, hear this roar against the iron gate,
A cry for freedom, loud and unafraid,
For in defiance, I shall truly create,
A life where every dream can be displayed.

29/29

The shadow that never leaves us

In every corner where the darkness clings,
And every step that silence softly sings,
A shadow follows, constant and profound,
A walk in the silence, ever bound.

It weaves through light and wraps around your soul,
A presence that no dawn can wholly console,
In moments bright or when the day is grey,
It lingers, darkly threading through the fray.

The shadow never leaves; it's always there,
A ghostly whisper in the cool night air,
It dances close with every fleeting breath,
A silent partner in the dance with death.

No matter how the sunlight warms the sky,
The shadow stays, a truth you can't deny,
It's shaped by every choice, each hidden scar,
A constant echo of the battles far.

In dreams and waking hours, it intertwines,
A part of you, through every dark design,
Yet in its presence, there's a strength revealed,
A reminder of the truths that life concealed.

For though the shadow stays and never parts,
It shapes the contours of your weary heart,
A mark of resilience in the endless night,
A testament to your enduring fight.

So let the shadow be a guide, not a curse,
A part of you that makes the journey terse,
For in its dark embrace, you'll find your way,
Through every night that bridges into day.

30/30

Flowers of blindness

In the garden where the sun refuses to touch,
Where shadows stretch and darkness clings too much,
There bloom the flowers of a sightless plight,
Their petals weep in endless, muted night.

Their colours, draped in veils of ashen grey,
Speak of a world where light has lost its way,
They wither in the silence, cold and stark,
A cruel reminder of the absent spark.

Their stems, though twisted by the unseen blight,
Hold up their blooms with fragile, waning might,
Each blossom's agony a twisted art,
A symbol of a broken, aching heart.

These flowers, though they grow, are steeped in pain,
Their beauty marred by shadows' harsh disdain,
They reach for solace that they'll never find,
A cruel joke of what's left behind.

In their blind existence, they bear the cost,
A testament to vision's bitter loss,
Their silent cries are etched in every leaf,
A mournful dance of dark, unending grief.

So let them rot where light will never fall,
In a garden cursed with shadows' bitter call,
For in their faded, silent, bitter bloom,
Lies the harsh truth of beauty's endless gloom.

31/31

Carpenter carving a heart

In the quiet of a sunlit shop,
Where shadows gently play,
A carpenter's hands begin to carve,
And shape the heart of clay.

The wood is rich, a timeless grain,
A canvas firm and true,
He sees the heart in every vein,
And breathes his spirit through.

With chisel sharp and steady hand,
He traces lines of love,
Each stroke a whisper, soft and grand,
As if guided from above.

The heart emerges, fine and clear,
From rough and rugged plane,
A symbol of a craft sincere,
A labour born of pain.

He sands away the jagged edge,
With patience, calm, and slow,
Smoothing each intricate pledge,
Until the feelings show.

In every curve, a story told,
In every grain, a sigh,
A heart that's carved from wood so old,
Yet tender as the sky.

His hands have shaped a work of art,
A gift from deep within,
A token of a lover's heart,
And where true love begins.

The final touch, a gentle varnish,
To seal the work of grace,
And as he steps back, there's a flourish,
Of tears upon his face.

For in the heart, he's carved so fine,
He sees his reflection,
A piece of love that's intertwined
With hope and deep affection.

So, in the quiet of his shop,
Where shadows gently part,
The carpenter has made a drop.
Of love—his crafted heart.

The heart now rests upon the shelf,
A treasure finely made,
Yet echoes of the woodman's self,
In every grain displayed.

It waits for hands to hold it close,
For eyes to see its grace,
A silent promise to propose
A love that time won't chase.

As twilight falls and shadows blend,
The carpenter sits still,
Reflecting on the heart, he penned
With tenderness and skill.

The grains of wood, the sculptor's touch,
Have woven tales anew,
And in this heart, he's given much.
Of dreams and hopes he knew.

But hearts are fragile, just like wood,
With knots and splinters deep,
And though he crafted as he could,
He knows its secrets keep.

For every love that's carved with care
Can hold both joy and pain,
And in its curves, a truth laid bare
Hearts, though strong, can strain.

Yet in the night, a soft light glows,
From lanterns hanging low,
The carpenter's heart, it gently shows.
A warmth that starts to grow.

He dreams of hands that'll hold this piece,
Of moments yet to come,
Where love and art find sweet release
In a life that's just begun.

The heart will journey far and wide,
In hands both young and old,
And in its travel, there'll reside.
The stories it has told.

For though the carpenter's work is done,
His heart remains within,
In every carved and polished one,
Love's quiet song begins.

So, in the quiet of the night,
Where lanterns softly gleam,
The heart he carved with all his might
Becomes a living dream.

32/32

Beads of lies

Strung upon a thread so fine,
A necklace of deceit,
Each bead tells a story, false design,
Where truth and falsehood meet.

They shimmer in the softest light,
A false and fleeting grace,
But underneath, a darker plight
Hides in their polished face.

The first bead whispers still,
A tale that's thin and sweet,
But as you wear it, with a thrill,
The truth begins to cheat.

The second bead, a touch of gold,
Conceals a crack of shame,
And every secret that's been told
It will taint the threads the same.

The third is red, a bold disguise,
A vivid, burning lie,
It flickers with the hope of skies.
But shadows cloud the eye.

As more are strung, the necklace grows,
A heavy, glittering chain,
And with each lie, a burden sows
A quiet, creeping pain.

The beads reflect a fractured light,
A shimmer cold and stark,
And in the depth of every night,
They leave a lasting mark.

33/33

Fought for the other

In Verona's shadowed streets they met,
Two hearts bound by fate's cruel thread,
Where love's sweet spark was quickly set
And dreams of joy were softly said.

She, a rose in summer's bloom,
With eyes like stars, so bright and clear,
He, a knight in midnight's gloom,
Whose heart beat only for her near.

Their love, a flame in tempest's storm,
Defied the world's relentless scorn,
And in their hearts, a bond was born,
A sacred vow, through night till morn.

Yet fate's dark hand, with cruel intent,
Was poised to part their tender souls,
And every hope and joy they spent
Was shadowed by the harshest tolls.

In whispered vows beneath the moon,
They pledged their hearts, forever true,
But time was fleeting, passing soon,
As destiny, its course withdrew.

A potion's dream, a dagger's plight,
A plan that faltered, love betrayed,
In twilight's final, somber light,
Their tragic end was deeply laid.

In tombs of stone, where silence lay,
Their love was sealed in death's cold grace,
And in their sleep, they found a way.
To leave behind the world's harsh face.

Yet though they left this earthly plane,
Their story lives, both fierce and bright,
A testament to love's sweet pain,
That echoes through the darkest night.

For in their tale, both lost and won,
A love was carved in time's stone,
And in the stars, their spirits spun,
A legacy that's all their own.

So let their names be whispers soft,
In every heart that dares to dream,
For Romeo and Juliet, aloft,
Are love's eternal, timeless theme.

34/34

The Blacksmith's dilemma

In the heart of a roaring forge,
Where shadows leap and play,
A blacksmith toils with tempered gorge,
On a blade of grim display.

The metal hums beneath his hand,
A Song of Fire and Steel,
Forging strength from rugged land,
In every strike and reel.

The knife he shapes is sharp and true,
Its edge a deadly line,
Designed for battles, fierce and new,
For vengeance to define.

Each hammer's fall, each molten pour,
Molds purpose into form,
Yet in the blacksmith's heart, a war
Brews in the evening's storm.

For though the blade is keenly wrought,
Its purpose dark and cold,
The blacksmith's soul, with mercy caught,
Begins to unfold.

He sees the future, bleak,
A path that's carved in strife,
And doubts begin to stir within.
The crucible of life.

The knife, a tool of death's brand,
Hangs heavy on his mind,
Yet in his heart, he makes a stand.
For peace that he will find.

With careful hands, he smooths the edge,
Polishing the steel,

Yet in his thoughts, a quiet pledge
Begins to heal gently.

He leaves the blade upon the shelf,
A symbol of his choice,
To rise above, to seek himself.
In reason's steady voice.

For though the knife is sharp and true,
Its purpose he denies,
And in the night, where shadows brew,
He chooses not to rise.

The blacksmith's art, though fierce and bold,
Becomes a tale of grace,
Of choosing mercy over gold,
And finding a new place.

So let the forge's fire blaze bright,
And echo through the land,
For in the blacksmith's tempered fight,
He chose a gentler hand.

35/35

What mask did you choose today?

Each morning, I don a silent guise,
A mask to hide my face,
In the mirror, behind the eyes,
A quiet, weary place.

The mask is stitched with threads of smiles,
Yet underneath, I know,
The truth is buried deep for miles,
Where only shadows go.

I walk through crowds with faces bright,
While inside, I'm shrouded, cold,
And though I laugh, my heart's not light,
It's silent, bruised, and old.

The mask conceals a trembling soul,
A heart that aches and yearns,
It plays a role, it takes its toll,
And in the quiet burns.

In conversations, voices blend,
Yet I'm a phantom here,
A stranger to the words I send,
A ghost that disappears.

The mask protects from prying eyes,
From truths too raw to share,
Yet in its cover, a disguise
That's worn with subtle care.

At night, I shed the face I wear,
And in the dark, I find
A mirror where I stare and stare,
At what I've left behind.

The mask is not just cloth or thread,
It's layers of pretense spun,

A shield for words I've never said,
A cover for the sun.

And as I face each dawning light,
With masks of many kinds,
I wonder if I'll find the sight.
Of truths that life unwinds.

So here I am, with masks arrayed,
A tapestry of guise,
Yet longing for a truth displayed.
Beyond these veiled ties.

Every day, I wear the mask,
And hide behind its grace,
But in my heart, I dare to ask.
When will I see my face?

36/36

Shattered trust

You said forever, now I'm alone,
Your promises turned to dust and stone.
Empty words, a bitter lie,
Left to weep and wonder why.

37/37

Fading Echoes

Once your love was my whole world,
Now, empty echoes, dreams unfurled.
Your touch was warmth, now just cold,
A cruel story left untold.

38/38

Forgotten Promises

You left with the words, "I'll stay,"
Now, those vows are swept away.
In your absence, pain remains,
A heart's betrayal, endless chains.

39/39

Hollow heart

In the chamber of my chest,
Echoes of a love that's gone,
A hollow heart, no longer blessed,
Where warmth and joy are drawn.

Silent whispers, space,
Where once beat a vibrant song,
Now it's a vacant, sorrowed place,
Where memories of us belong.

40/40

Thief of joy

In gardens where our hearts once bloomed,
Comparison creeps unseen,
It steals the light where dreams were groomed,
And dims the vibrant sheen.

It whispers lies of what's not mine,
And shadows what is real,
Turning joy to a hollow sign,
Where envy starts to steal.

Each moment lost to doubt and sigh,
A treasure turned to sand,
As joy's pure light begins to die,
In the thief's cruel hand.

41/41

Oh, here the sky cries too.

No rainbow's promise, no golden hue, just endless lament in the sky's deep blue. If the sky weeps, its sorrow stays, A silent vigil through endless days.

42/42

Be someone's pulse

Be someone's heart, where love takes flight,
A tender pulse in the quiet night.
A rhythm that beats with passion's grace,
A haven where their dreams embrace.

Be the warmth in their every breath,
A comfort through the shadow of death.
In moments of joy or deep despair,
Be the heartbeat that lingers there.

Be the melody in their silent tune,
A whisper soft as a lover's moon.
In every touch, in every glance,
Be the heartbeat that ignites romance.

Be the core where their hopes reside,
An endless love, a wide love.
In every sigh and gentle touch,
Be the heart that means so much.

Be the rhythm of their sweetest dreams,
A pulse where every star gleams.
In the dance of time, both slow and fast,
Be the heartbeat that forever lasts.

For in being their heart, so true,
You craft a love that's always new.
A pulse that binds their soul to yours,
In a romance that forever endures.

Without you

Without your smile, the world feels grey,
A shadow falls where light should play.
Without your touch, the day is cold,
A story half-told, a love left untold.

Without your laugh, the silence speaks,
A void where joy and warmth once peeked.
Without you here, my heart's adrift,
In the quiet, longing for your gift.

44/44

Add

You can't add days to your life, they say,
Just watch the moments slip away.
The hours fade, the years drift by,
With empty echoes of goodbye.

You can't stretch time or halt its flight,
Each day dissolves into the night.
With every dream that slips from reach,
Life's fleeting lessons are hard to teach.

You can't reclaim what's lost in time,
No second chance, no reason, rhyme.
In the quiet, shadows fall,
A reminder of the days that call.

45/45

Live now

In the dance of fleeting time so bright,
Live in the moment, and bask in its light.
Embrace the now with tender grace,
Where life's pure essence finds its place.

Let not the past or future's call,
Distract you from the present's thrall.
In each breath's gentle, rhythmic sweep,
Find joy that in the now does keep.

Time drifts by on silken streams,
Tomorrow fades like distant dreams.
So, savour the day as shadows play,
In the warmth of now, let your heart stay.

Live in the moment, where eternity sighs,
In the whisper of the now, let your spirit rise.
For moments are fleeting, like a soft, sweet song,
Yet in the present, life's true grace belongs.

46/46

Portrait of someone close

In her gaze, a universe unfolds,
A charm she has, a love untold.
Her eyes, like stars in velvet night,
Hold a warmth that feels so right.

Her smile, a whisper soft and sweet,
Turns ordinary moments to a heart's retreat.
A charm she has, like moonlight's glow,
That makes the deepest feelings grow.

Her laughter dances through the air,
A melody of joy, beyond compare.
A charm she has that binds the soul,
A love that makes the broken whole.

In each caress, a timeless grace,
A charm she has in every trace.

She weaves romance with every sigh,
A charm she has that makes hearts fly.
In her presence, dreams come alive,
A love so deep, it will forever thrive.

47/47

Now or never
This is pretty much it. Now or never,
So be it, or let it stay forever.
Make it count. No lives respawn,
Listen to your heart; respond.
48/48

Slaughtered child

I once had a wild child inside of me,

Lost it in a parody,

It never felt like an eternity,

It's lost and gone for us to see.

49/49

Meant to be

In the maze of life, where paths intertwine,
There's freedom in wandering, in losing time.
No map can confine us, no compass can bind,
In being lost, we find what we seek inside.

In the depths of the unknown, our hearts find grace,
Embracing the journey, we discover our place.
So wander with wonder, let your spirit be free,
For in being lost, you're truly just where you're meant to be.

50/50

Tore it apart

In the harsh glare of the broken light,
We see the end of our endless fight.
What once was love is now a scar,
A bitter truth that cuts too far.

For us to see the wreckage we've made,
To confront the lies and the trust that's frayed.
In the rubble of promises, cold and stark,
We face the truth in the silence and dark.

The dreams we shared now feel so cheap,
Echoes of laughter, now shadows we weep.
You were a storm, I was the calm,
Now, we're left with this hollow psalm.

In the ruins of what we once claimed,
We're left with a love that's bruised and maimed.
For us to see the wounds that run deep,
We face the ruin of the vows we couldn't keep.

The pain is sharp, a cruel reminder,
Of how our love became a slow grinder.
For us to see what's left in the wake,
We tear apart the hearts we can't remake.

51/51

Sarcastic society

You, welcome to the circus where the clowns run the show,
Every headline's a disaster, every truth's got a low blow.
They sell us illusions like they're flipping the script,
In this rat race of misery, we're all getting ripped.

The rich get richer, yeah, and the poor just bleed,
While the powers feed us fake news and greed.
Watch the puppets dance, watch 'em pull all the strings,
In this toxic pool where corruption's king.

We're caught in the trap, where the lies never end,
Fake smiles and double-talk from the suits that pretend.
They say we're free, but it's a damn joke,
In a world full of smoke and mirrors, we choke.

Preachers of progress, yeah, but where's the change?
They've got us spinning in circles, just a mindless exchange.
So take a look around at the mess they create,
It's a shit society, yeah, and it's time to break the gate.

The system's rigged, the deck is stacked,
And we're left to pick up the pieces of the dreams they've cracked.
Rise up, stand tall, it's a fight we have to see,
In this shitty world, it's time for you and me.

Check it, this is the mess they've made,
A twisted reality where truth gets betrayed.
We're fed a steady diet of the lies they spew,
In a world where the shady rule and the honest are screwed.

See the fat cats in their ivory towers,
Pushing propaganda while they siphon the powers.
We're shackled by headlines that twist and turn,
In this broken system where the lessons burn.

Corporate puppets pull strings with greed,
Feeding us crap while we plead and we bleed.

They say it's progress, but it's a sleazy show,
Where every dollar's a cut, every truth's a blow.

We're caught in a loop, a cycle of deceit,
Where the powerful laugh while we're down on our knees.
Look around, man, the streets are rife,
With the broken promises and the shards of our life.

Politicians and media, they're all in on the con,
Playing a game while the real fights are gone.
It's a spectacle of pain, a show of disgrace,
Where the truth's an illusion in a high-stakes race.

But we're rising from the ashes, got a fire in our veins,
Going to tear down the system, break these chains.
They've made a mess, but we're here to clean,
In this shit society, we're the ones to redeem.

So, get up, get ready, it's time to act,
To stand up, fight back, and hit them with the facts.
In this world of deception, let's clear the debris,
For a future where the truth's not a distant fantasy.

52/52

A mindset which I don't mind

Step into my head, it's a war zone,
Mind's a battlefield, and I'm fighting all alone.
Thoughts like grenades, they're exploding with a bang,
In this messed-up carnival where sanity's a prank.

I'm trapped in my skull, a mental prison cell,
Where every self-doubt's a demon and every echo's hell.
Psyche's a minefield, a landmine of pain,
Every step's a gamble in this mental hurricane.

Face the mirror, it's a cracked, distorted lens,
Reflecting all my demons, all my twisted sins.
They say I'm free, but I'm chained in my own mind,
Locked in a cage, where the truth's hard to find.

Screaming at the void, but it just laughs back,
In this circus where sanity's slack.
Mental tornado, spinning out of control,
Wrestling with shadows, I'm losing my soul.

They preach "rise up," but my chains are too tight,
In a world where I'm drowning, suffocating in night.
Shit mindset's a prison, and the bars are steel cold,
Fighting inner demons while my story's retold.

But I'm coming out swinging, won't be kept in the dark,
Going to torch this mindset and leave a blazing mark.
In this mental battlefield, I'm claiming my right,
Turning rage into power, going to burn through the night.

I'm a fighter, a warrior, breaking through the fray,
Going to take back my mind; no more living this way.
In the wreckage of thought where the shadows once lay,
I'll rise from the ashes, redefine the fray.

53/53

Delusional illusions.

In the mosaic of the crowd where illusions weave,
The faces blend, and the deceivers deceive.
Among the voices that whisper and shout,
Lie the shallow souls who know nothing about.

Their smiles are masks, their words just dust,
In the realm of the empty where trust turns to rust.
In the theatre of where shadows dance,
We're haunted by echoes of a fleeting glance.

They parade as saints, but their hearts are hollow,
In the maze where the real can't follow.
Their promises are whispers in a tempest of lies,
Crafted with care to mask the disguise.

In the spotlight of the false, they strut and they claim,
Yet beneath the façade is a soul bound in shame.
Their values are mirrors, reflecting the dark,
In the gallery of masks, they leave a stark mark.

We tread through their world with eyes open wide,
In the ocean where the genuine hides.
For in the depth of their schemes, we find the shallow sea,
The art of deception in its raw, empty plea.

So, we navigate the maze, where the pretenders reside,
With hearts made of iron and truths set aside.
For in the landscape of falsehood, where shit people dwell,
We seek the light of honesty amidst the fake and the swell.

Step into the ring where the fakes all reside,
In the circus of deceit where the truth's denied.
Their smiles are plastered, their charm's a disguise,
In the theatre of bullshit where honesty dies.

They talk a big game, but their words are hollow,
Walking contradictions, got no real follow.

Their laughter's a facade, their friendship a scam,
In the wasteland of trust where the real gets damned.

Their promises are smoke, their values are thin,
In the battle where the genuine's pinned.
Watch them strut and preen with their phony charade,
In a masquerade ball where integrities betrayed.

They play the hero, but their deeds are weak,
In the land of the fake where the genuine's bleak.
They're hustling illusions, spinning webs of deceit,
While the truth's buried deep beneath their deceitful beat.

They say they got your back, but their loyalty's thin,
In this savage game where the real's wearing thin.
They're puppets and marionettes in a cruel, hollow show,
With strings pulled by lies in the darkness below.

So, here's a middle finger to the fake-ass crowd,
In a world full of noise where the truth gets drowned.
I'm cutting through the bullshit, no time for the phony,
In a realm of deception, I'm standing alone.

We see through the masks, through the lies and the games,
In this battlefield of bullshit where nothing's the same.
So forget the pretenders and the games that they play,
I'm forging my path, clearing the debris of their sway.

54/54

Pain isn't powering

Pain isn't powerful, it's just a fleeting guest,
It knocks you down hard, but don't let it be your test.
It's a chapter in the struggle, just another fight,
But you're the hero of the story, shining through the night.

Pain's a loudmouth bully, tries to steal your fire,
But you're the beast, the force, the one they can't tire.
It's a glitch in the system, a bump in the road,
But you're the engine of resilience, never slowing the load.

Yeah, it's heavy, it's gritty, like a weight on your chest,
But pain's just a moment, not a permanent quest.
You rise from the ashes, turn the hurt into might,
With every scar you earn, you're winning the fight.

Don't let the shadows fool you, don't let them claim your soul,
Pain is just a pit stop on the way to your goal.
You're a powerhouse, a dynamo, the truth they can't deny,
In the face of the struggle, you're reaching for the sky.

So, when the pain's knocking, and you're feeling the burn,
Just remember, it's a lesson, a point you'll discern.
You're stronger than the hurt, you're blazing your own trail,
In the game of life, pain's just a gust in the gale.

55/55

Hate is a choice

Hate is a choice, it's not some cosmic curse,
It's a weapon you wield, a way to make it worse.
You pick up the grudge, you let the venom seep,
In this mental warfare, it's your soul you're deep.

Hate's a poison you brew in the pit of your chest,
It's a self-made prison where your peace gets suppressed.
You're the puppet master pulling strings of despair,
In the battlefield of emotions, you going to be aware.

You can let it consume, let it twist up your brain,
Or you can flip the switch and break free from the chains.
Hate's a weak excuse for the battles you lose,
In the war of the mind, you choose what you use.

In this world of chaos, where anger's a trend,
You're the one who decides how the story will end.
You can feed the rage, let it burn and destroy,
Or you can rise above, let the peace be your ploy.

So, when the fury's blazing and you're ready to snap,
Remember, you're the one who controls the trap.
You got the power, you got the voice,
In the symphony of life, hate is a choice.

So, drop the venom, stop the endless fight,
In the mirror of your soul, make the wrongs turn right.
You're the author of the anger, the master of the noise,
In the war for your spirit, hate's just a choice.

56/56

Hurt both of us

We're wrecked in this mess, hearts shattered and torn,
Caught in a storm where love's left us worn.
Every word's a dagger, every silence a scar,
In this tragic play, we've both fallen too far.

You're in your corner, while I'm lost in this fight,
Two broken souls drifting in the night.
Every fight's a wound, every glance a reminder,
That we're both on the edge, with no one to find us.

We're swinging through shadows, trying to find the light,
Two fractured hearts, struggling through the night.
Each cut, each bruise, a mark of our regret,
In this storm of heartbreak, we're both caught in the net.

Battling our ghosts, haunted by what we've lost,
Two souls, same pain, but at what cost?
We're drowning in memories where love used to blaze,
In the ruins of us, lost in a daze.

So let's lay down our grudges, try to heal these wounds,
In this shattered love, where hope's been exhumed.
Both of us hurt, but we're trapped in this bind,
In the wreckage of us, can we leave the past behind?

57/57

Safe at shore

A boat rests at the shore, where the land kisses the sea,
But it's not meant for this haven, it's built for the open spree.
Anchored in tranquillity, its mission stands deferred,
For its heart is wild, its spirit undeterred.

The shore whispers comfort in a quiet, soothing tone,
Yet the boat is restless, for it's never truly alone.
Its hull, though weathered, yearns for the roaring waves,
Not to linger in calm, but to conquer and be brave.

The shoreline may cradle, may offer a fleeting peace,
But the boat's true calling is where the tempests never cease.
It's crafted for the storm, for the dance of wind and tide,
To cut through the chaos, with the sea as its guide.

The horizon calls fiercely, where the wild waves crash,
It's not a place for rest but for a bold, daring dash.
The boat dreams of the battle, of cresting every swell,
It's a vessel of adventure with untold tales to tell.

Rest here is an interlude, a pause in the grand fight,
Yet the boat's soul is yearning for the waves' fierce might.
For it's meant to roam the oceans, to ride through every squall,
Not to linger in stillness, but to heed the ocean's call.

So let it not be anchored, let it break from this shore,
For the boat's destiny lies in the waves it must explore.
In the vast expanse of water, where the wild currents blaze,
It's there the boat will find its true and fearless ways.

58/58

**If it was meant to be easy, then everyone would have been
on the other side of work.**

Gamble it off

I'd gamble life, place my bet on the unknown,
Push my chips to the centre, where the seeds are sown.
In the casino of existence, with its stakes so high,
I'd wager on the wild card and let the dice fly.

I'd roll the dice with fate, risk it all for the thrill,
Embrace the unpredictable, bend to destiny's will.
For the comfort of certainty is a cage, not a prize,
And the heart finds its rhythm where the wild chance lies.

I'd gamble on the sunrise, on dreams that blaze and burn,
Bet on the roads less travelled, where the lessons turn.
In the game of life, where the odds are never clear,
I'd stake my claim on passion, face down every fear.

Life's not a safe bet, it's a gamble every day,
With fortunes made and lost in a high-stakes play.
So I'll bet on the heartbeat, the fire that drives the soul,
In the whirl of the roulette, where the dice take their toll.

Let the cards be dealt, let the numbers align,
I'll embrace the gamble, let the stars define.
For in the risk lies the story, in the chance, the true prize,
I'd gamble life's adventure beneath these boundless skies.

59/59

Roller coaster

Strap in tight, love, for this ride's about to start,
We're on a roller coaster, with adrenaline in our hearts.
Through the loops and the turns, through the highs and the lows,
We're screaming together, where the wild emotion flows.

Feel the rush as we climb, hand in hand, side by side,
In the ascent of our passion, with nowhere to hide.
The thrill of the drop, as we plunge into the blue,
In this ride of romance, every twist is new.

The peaks are our triumphs, the valleys our fears,
We're laughing through the wind, drying each other's tears.
The speed of our love, with its moments so bright,
In the rush of our journey, we dance through the night.

We're coasting through the thrills, in the flashes of light,
Every loop is a promise, and every turn feels right.
In the chaos and the calm, in the roar and the hush,
We're united in the thrill, in the beautiful rush.

When the ride comes to a stop and the lights start to fade,
We'll cherish the memories, the highs, and the cascade.
For in the heart of the journey, where the love's truly grand,
We've braved every twist together, hand in hand.

60/60

A Knot, not meant to be untied

We're a knot, tightly bound, in the weave of our love's thread,
A twist of fate and passion, where our hearts are led.
Through the highs and the lows, in the struggle and the strife,
We're tangled together, bound by the essence of life.

The knot might pull and strain, in the storms we face,
Yet it's forged with the strength of a sacred embrace.
In the heat of our battles, in the dark of our plight,
Our bond holds unbroken, a beacon of light.

Each twist and turn of the rope tells of battles won and lost,
Of the price of our journey, of the struggles we've crossed.
In the tapestry of our love, where the patterns are entwined,
We're a knot that's resilient in the grand design.

When the world tests our limits, when shadows start to fall,
The knot we've tied remains, standing tall through it all.
For it's not just a bond, but a testament so true,
To the depth of our connection, to the love we pursue.

So let the trials come, let the challenges rise,
Our knots are not meant to be untied, not to compromise.
In the struggle and the heartache, in the fight we endure,
We're bound by a love that's steadfast and pure.

In the weave of our struggle, through every joy and pain,
This knot's a symbol of love that will always remain.
For in the dance of our passion, where the destinies blend,
Our knot stays unbroken until the very end.

61/61

No spectacles

I'm living life without spectacles, no filters on my sight,
Seeing clear through the chaos, cutting through the blight.
No rose-tinted glasses, no illusions to deceive,
Just raw, unvarnished truth, in the way I believe.

62/62

Headphones on

In a world of noise, where voices collide,
I slip into silence, let my heart be my guide.
With headphones sealed tight, the hum fades away,
In this cocoon of sound, I find my way.

The chatter of the masses, just static to me,
I'm tuned to my rhythm, where I'm meant to be.
Every beat's a whisper from my soul's deep well,
Echoes of my truth in this self-made shell.

No external distractions, just the pulse of my dreams,
Lost in the melody, or so it seems.
With every note, my heart charts a course,
Navigating life with a powerful force.

The world may scream, but I'm wrapped in a zone,
In the clarity of silence, I'm never alone.
Each beat in my ear, a guide through the night,
In the symphony of solitude, I embrace my light.

With headphones on, the outside fades to grey,
Here in my sanctuary, I find my way.
In this sacred space where only my heart can lead,
I find strength and solace and fulfill my own needs.

In the hush of the night, where whispers dissolve,
I slip into silence and let my thoughts evolve.
Headphones on tight, a shield from the roar,
A sanctuary crafted on my heart's own floor.

Each note is a beacon, cutting through the haze,
Guiding me gently through the labyrinthine maze.
Voices of the world may clamour and clash,
But in this cocoon, my dreams are free to splash.

No outside echoes, just the rhythm of my core,
In this symphony of solitude, I yearn for more.

The beat of my heart syncs with the song in my ear,
Creating a haven where my path becomes clear.

The world outside is a cacophony of sound,
But within these headphones, peace is found.
Melodies weave through the fabric of my mind,
Crafting a world where I find my true self.

Here, I am the maestro, the composer of my fate,
In the quiet symphony, I deliberate, contemplate.
With every beat that resonates, a story unfolds,
Of a soul navigating life, fearless and bold.

With headphones on, the universe fades to grey,
Within this private concert, I drift away.
In this haven of sound, where only I belong,
I'm empowered, I'm free, in the rhythm of my song.

63/63

Faults and Love

In the garden where our hearts entwine,
Faults and love both softly fall,
Imperfect blooms in the moonlight's shine,
All the truths that bind us all.

Faults, like pebbles in a stream,
Ripple through our silent grace,
While love, like sunlight's gentle beam,
Illuminating each hidden place.

Yet in these cracks, where shadows play,
Love's embrace is warm and bright,
For faults reveal, in their way,
The depth and strength of love's true light.

Love finds beauty in the scars,
In the rough and tender parts,
It sees beyond the surface mars,
And cherishes our hearts.

So let the shadows dance and weave,
Let faults and love entwine,
For through our flaws, we truly weave.
A tapestry divine.

64/64

Falls on you

When troubles fall upon your soul,
Like tempest rain from skies above,
The heavens weep in gentle toll,
For every tear reflects their love.

The clouds, they gather, dark and deep,
To cradle sorrows, soft and wide,
And as they weep, they quietly sweep.
The heartache from your weary side.

Each drop that falls from skies so high,
Is not just rain but solace sent,
A tender sigh from the boundless sky,
To mend the heart where troubles went.

In every storm and thunder's roar,
The heavens share your silent plight,
For in their tears, you'll find the more,
A promise of the coming light.

So, when the sky weeps for your pain,
Know it's love that falls with rain,
For every cloud that darkly cries,
Is but a prelude to clear skies

65/65

Collect Dust

Life's a recorder, always on replay,
Chasing dreams, but they slip away,
Piles of regrets on the bookshelf's edge,
Words of wisdom? Nah, just a broken pledge.

I collect dust on this old desk,
Memories and scars, yeah, they're grotesque,
Life's a hurricane, I'm just the debris,
Stuck in the whirlwind, can't you see?

Dust gathers in the corners, deep,
Like the secrets that I never speak,
Cracked dreams and faded glory,
Pages from a half-told story.

Got trophies on the mantle, just for show,
But they gather dust, and so does my soul,
Success is a myth, man, it's all a lie,
When you're staring at the ceiling, asking why.

I'm a warrior with rust, yeah, I'm battle-worn,
Dreams in the attic, where they're tattered and torn,
But I'm still here, fighting through the muck,
Dust may settle, but I'm never stuck.

So, I wipe the grime and clear the haze,
Rising from the ashes, setting new blaze,
Collecting dust, but I'm more than grime,
Turning wreckage into rhythm, it's my time.

I'd **flirt** with death if it was you. Flirting is an overstatement, but still, you know.

67/67

Why can't I?

In the corridors of my mind, I'm trapped, can't you see?
Every step I take, it's like they're burying me,
Dreams heavy on my shoulders, dragging me down,
Trying to lift off the ground, but I'm stuck in this town.

Why can't I break free from these chains of doubt?
Every time I try to soar, it's like I'm strung out,
Climbing mountains high, but the summit's out of sight,
In the mirror, I'm a fighter, but I'm losing the fight.

Why can't I rise from these shadows, from the dark?
Voices in my head telling me to depart,
Grinding and hustling, but the doubt pulls tight,
Screaming at the sky, "Why can't I get it right?"

Why can't I trust the process and endure the pain?
Every victory feels hollow, every loss feels like a chain,
Battling demons fierce, keeping me low,
Feeling like I'm caught in this perpetual flow.

Why can't I see the light, the spark in my soul?
Every setback hits hard, taking its toll,
Clawing through the darkness, seeking a spark,
But self-doubt's a shadow, leaving its mark.

So, I'm pouring out my fears, putting ink to the page,
Trying to break free from this invisible cage,
In the silence, I'm fighting, searching for a way,
To turn self-doubt into strength, to seize the day.

No more "Why can't I?" just "Watch me defy,"
Turning self-doubt into wings, reaching for the sky,
From shadows and pain, I'll emerge and fly,
Transforming every question into a resolute "I."

68/68

Find beauty in every flaw and grace in every imperfection; if it
was meant to be, it will be.

69/69

Told someone

In the hush of twilight, where dreams softly glow,
I've told her things no one else could know,
Secrets like whispers on a breeze so light,
Shared in the tender stillness of the night.

In the warmth of her gaze, where stars gently gleam,
I've revealed the depths of my most cherished dream,
With each heartfelt confession, each soft, tender sigh,
We've painted our love beneath the velvet sky.

Her touch, a sanctuary where shadows dissolve,
In her arms, my truths and fears gently evolve,
In moments of stillness, where time stands still,
I've bared my soul, revealed every thrill.

She knows my heart's corners, the fears I've concealed,
The dreams that in darkness have softly revealed,
In the secret garden of our shared embrace,
I've given her my soul, my heart's sacred space.

So, in the quiet of love's unspoken lore,
We've shared a bond that goes to the core,
In the intimacy of trust, where our secrets intertwine,
I've told her things no one else could define.

70/70

If perfection is no one's piece of cake, so is moderation. I'd argue
that moderation is the pinnacle of perfection

71/71

Learn to accept fate as we age, but still, why do we deny reality?

Why?

Am I dreaming?

Am I dreaming, or is this scene real?
Got my mind spinning, can't tell what I feel,
Life's a twisted carnival, I'm stuck on the ride,
Every turn's a gamble, with nowhere to hide.

Is this reality or just a wild charade?
Lost in my thoughts like a mind parade,
The world's a mirror, but it's cracked and stained,
Reflections of a psyche that's breaking and strained.

Every beat of my heart, like a ticking time bomb,
Got me questioning every line and every song,
Caught in the middle of a lucid dream haze,
Is this my life, or am I just a phase?

Reality's slipping through my fingers like sand,
Grasping at shadows, trying to understand,
In the chaos of my thoughts, where nightmares play,
I'm asking the universe, "Is this where I stay?"

Feel like a puppet, tangled in strings,
Wondering if I'm trapped in the wrong rings,
The mirror's got cracks, reflecting my fears,
Tell me, am I dreaming, or are these just tears?

72/72

Am I still young?

They say I'm still too young, like I'm stuck in a phase,
But I'm hustling hard, and I'm setting the blaze,
Got a fire in my chest, is no slowing down,
While they're doubting my moves, I'm owning this town.

They see a kid with a dream, thinking I'm too green,
But I'm going through the scenes, like a storm unseen,
Yeah, I'm raw, and I'm real, got my eyes on the prize,
You can see the hunger burning in these young eyes.

73/73

Wicked mind

In the cavern of a wicked mind,
Where shadows twist and secrets bind,
The thoughts like serpents, sly and sleek,
Whisper sins that angels seek.

A labyrinth where nightmares crawl,
In twisted dreams that heed no call,
Each corridor a silent scream,
A haunt of dark, forbidden dream.

The intellect, both sharp and cruel,
Plays in shadows, breaks the rule,
Crafts illusions in the dark,
With wicked art, a serpent's mark.

Desires churn in depths concealed,
In the shadowed corners, unwrapped,
A tempest brewed of murk and sin,
Where light dares not to venture in.

Yet in this maze of grim delight,
Where reason falters, lost to night,
There lies a beauty, dark and strange,
In every wicked, shifting change.

For even in the twisted mind,
Where virtue's voice is hard to find,
There's a poetry in shadows cast,
In the fleeting light that's outclassed.

So, ponder well the wicked's art,
The darkened realms where secrets start,
For in the depth of shadows' fold,
Lie stories dark and truths untold.

74/74

Brewed fresh

In a world where shadows twist and play,
Lies brew fresh like morning's grey,
A fragrant deceit in whispered tones,
Veiled truths are hidden, and secrets sown.

They simmer softly in the night,
Like tea leaves curling out of sight,
A brew of stories spun with care,
Shrouded in a false veneer.

Each word a sip, a taste so sweet,
Yet leaves a bitterness beneath,
A mask that smiles, a gentle guise,
Crafted well to hide the lies.

They steep in hearts and cloud the mind,
Warping truth, where doubt is blind,
A potion brewed with subtle art,
To twist the truth and play the part.

The cup of lies, so smooth and warm,
Might charm the soul but leaves it torn,
A fleeting comfort, false delight,
That fades away with the morning's light.

So, when you taste that fresh deceit,
Remember well the bitter beat,
For in each lie, a truth may hide,
But the heart knows when it's been denied.

Let truth be clear, a dawn's pure stream,
To cleanse the palate, end the scheme,
For lies may brew fresh, soft, and sly,
But they unravel when the dawn draws at night.

75/75

Kindle my interest

In a meadow where the sunlight plays,
I've come to share a dream today,
To kindle in your heart a spark,
A gentle flame to leave its mark.

Imagine, if you will, the dawn,
With golden light upon the lawn,
Where every blade of grass and leaf
Whispers of belief.

Picture a brook that winds its way,
Through fields where wildflowers sway,
Their colours bright beneath the sky,
A palette where your dreams can fly.

I'll paint for you a scene so rare,
Where time seems paused in the still air,
Where shadows dance and sunlight gleams,
And life is woven into dreams.

The lark above sings pure and clear,
A melody that draws you near,
Its notes are like whispers in the breeze,
Enticing thoughts with gentle ease.

In this quiet, sacred space,
You'll find a warmth, a soft embrace,
A spark of wonder, pure and true,
That kindles interest deep in you.

So, take this vision, hold it tight,
Let it unfold in morning light,
And let the flame within you grow,
As you discover what I know.

Me being a toy

A toy, though simple, has its part,
In mending hearts and warming art,
So, as ye play and laugh away,
Remember me, the toy, I pray.

For in this fleeting, gentle role,
I find my place, I find my soul,
And though my form may be but small,
In each child's joy, I stand tall.

77/77

Ease the pain

In quiet shadows, whispers weave,
A tender balm for hearts that grieve.
Like softest rain on thirsty ground,
In gentle moments, peace is found.

The weight of sorrow, heavy, dense,
Can cloak the soul in silence, tense.
Yet through the cracks, a light will creep,
A fragile hope that stirs from sleep.

Take a breath, slow down the racing heart,
Let stillness hold you, a work of art.
With every sigh, release the ache,
A fragile thread, a promise made.

In nature's arms, the wildflower sways,
Each petal whispers of brighter days.
A touch of sun, a breeze's grace,
Can soothe the wounds we dare not face.

Feel the earth beneath your feet,
A reminder that life's pulse is sweet.
The gentle rustle of leaves above,
A symphony of life, a song of love.

Let laughter rise like morning's light,
Break through the dark, embrace the fight.
For in the laughter, pain finds ease,
A moment's joy, a gentle breeze.

The echoes of joy may fade away,
Yet memories linger, come what may.
In shared stories, we weave a thread,
A tapestry of love that's gently spread.

Embrace the scars, let stories flow,
For in the depths, we learn to grow.

Each tear is a testament, each wound a guide,
A path toward healing, where hope can reside.

Remember the warmth of a friend's embrace,
The comfort found in a familiar place.
In the company of those who understand,
The weight of pain becomes less grand.

Through every storm, the heart must brave,
The depths of sorrow, the rise from the grave.
Yet in that struggle, strength is born,
A resilient spirit, beautifully worn.

So, when the world feels cold and grey,
And shadows linger, clouding the way,
Reach for the light that flickers within,
A spark of courage, where hope can begin.

For pain is a journey, not just a chain,
A fleeting visitor, though it may remain.
In time, the heart learns to dance once more,
To find the beauty in what's in store.

With each passing moment, let kindness reign,
Embrace the laughter, ease the pain.
In the tapestry of life, woven tight,
May love and healing guide you to light.

78/78

Sailor loving shore

Upon the waves, a sailor roams,
His heart is adrift, far from his home.
With salt-kissed skin and windswept hair,
Yet deep within, he holds a prayer.

The ocean's call, a siren's song,
Draws him to depths where dreams belong.
But beneath the vast, cerulean hue,
Lies a longing for the land he knew.

For though he dances with the tide,
There's a yearning in him he cannot hide.
Each cresting wave, a fleeting kiss,
But it's the shore he truly misses.

The blue, so bold, holds him tight,
Yet there's a darkness in its light.
He craves the warmth of sunlit sand,
The gentle touch of a waiting hand.

The endless azure, a prison vast,
A beautiful cage, where shadows are cast.
He sails the seas with a heart so sore,
For it's the shore he loves, forevermore.

Oh, how he longs for the rustling trees,
The whispers of the wind, the buzzing bees.
The colours of dusk, the amber glow,
While the blue of the sea remains his foe.

He dreams of evenings, the sky aflame,
While the ocean's blue, it feels so tame.
Its endlessness, a daunting fright,
In the quiet of dusk, he seeks the light.

He'll chase the horizon, but his heart will steer
Back to the shore, where love is near.

For every wave that breaks and sways,
It's the land that holds his heart ablaze.

So let him sail, a wanderer bold,
With stories of seas and treasures untold.
But when the stars light the tranquil shore,
He'll find his peace, forevermore.

79/79

Frankenstein deserves to be loved.

In a world of stone and steel,
A creature born, a heart to feel.
Stitched from shadows, parts combined,
Yet in his chest, a soul aligned.

Born of ambition, a spark ignites,
Yet cast aside, he fades from sight.
A being longing, yearning for grace,
In the mirror of man, he found no place.

With every glance, a gaze of dread,
Misunderstood, his spirit bled.
He roamed the earth, a silent plea,
"Is there no love, no place for me?"

Victor, creator, with dreams so grand,
Forgot the heart that needs a hand.
For in that frame, so wild and free,
Lived a desire to simply be.

He wandered fields where flowers sway,
Imagined love in the light of day.
Yet every face, a frown, a scream,
A shattered heart, a broken dream.

"Deserved to be loved," the echoes cry,
For every monster has a reason why.
In every heartbeat, a wish to belong,
A melody lost, yet yearning for song.

In the depths of night, when silence reigned,
He sought a bond but found only pain.
The shadows whispered, the winds conspired,
For love, he longed; for kindness, he tired.

Yet in his anguish, there burned a flame,
A hope that one would share his name.

To find a friend in the darkest hour,
To blossom forth, a fragrant flower.

So let us see beyond the guise,
For every creature has its ties.
In the heart of the monster, a wish so pure,
A longing for love, a need to endure.

He deserved a chance, a gentle hand,
To walk with grace upon the land.
For in the depths of every night,
Lies a yearning for love's soft light.

So, when we look at the faces that fright,
Let's seek the love hidden from sight.
For even in darkness, we can discover,
All deserve love from one another.

80/80

Doll's lament

In a quiet room where shadows fall,
A porcelain doll stands, abandoned and small.
Once bright and cherished, her eyes would gleam,
Now dulled by the silence, lost in a dream.

Once I was held, cradled with care,
Dressed in fine silks, I danced through the air.
Laughter and whispers filled every day,
But now, those sweet moments have faded away.

The hands that once played have turned to the past,
A fleeting affection, too fragile to last.
I recall the warmth of a child's embrace,
Now, echoes of memories linger in place.

I've seen the light fade from joyous eyes,
As laughter turned quiet, and love turned to lies.
A heart once so tender, now heavy with pain,
I stand here alone, in this dollhouse of rain.

The games we played are a distant refrain,
A symphony lost in the shadows of rain.
I long for the touch that would make me feel whole,
But here in the silence, I search for my soul.

Dust gathers softly on my fragile frame,
Each day that I wait feels like a cruel game.
I'm trapped in this stillness, a ghost of the past,
A memory fading, a love that won't last.

Oh, to be loved, to be played with again,
To feel the warmth of a heart that won't wane.
But the world has moved on, and I'm left behind,
A heartbroken doll, with dreams unrefined.

If only the child would return to my side,
To brush back the dust and let laughter abide.

But here I remain, in this shadowy space,
Yearning for joy, for a familiar face.

So, I stand here alone, in this room so stark,
A doll once adored is now lost in the dark.
With each passing moment, I feel love decay,
A heart made of porcelain, broken and frayed.

Yet still, I hold hope in this silent despair,
That one day a child will return with a care.
For even a doll, with a heart made of clay,
Deserves to be loved, not left in dismay.

81/81

Handcuffed to my heart

In the quiet of the night, when shadows play,
I find my heart handcuffed, yet joy leads the way.
Bound to the warmth of your tender embrace,
Each link in this chain feels like love's sacred space.

You were the spark that ignited my fire,
A whirlwind of passion, my deepest desire.
With every heartbeat, I dance in your light,
Handcuffed to a dream that feels perfectly right.

Your laughter lingers like whispers of air,
A melody so soft that it erases despair.
In the depths of my soul, I'm anchored to you,
A love that's unyielding, steadfast, and true.

Together we wander through twilight's sweet haze,
In a world full of wonder, lost in a gaze.
Each moment we share, a treasure we find,
Handcuffed to a feeling that forever binds.

Though chains may be heavy, they shimmer with gold,
For in this connection, a story unfolds.
With every challenge, our hearts intertwine,
In the dance of our love, we're perfectly aligned.

So let the world fade, let the night draw near,
For I'm handcuffed to love, with you always here.
In this beautiful prison, I've come to know,
That with you beside me, my heart will only grow.

No need to escape, for this bond is divine,
A handcuff of passion, your heart locked in mine.
In the depths of the night, where shadows depart,
I'm forever enchanted, handcuffed to my heart.

What if the door which you are **afraid** to open is just shut, not
locked?

The Beggar's Coins

He sits, bent low beneath the weight of years,
A shadow draped in tattered robes, his face
A canvas marked with time and silent tears,
The lines of struggle were etched in every trace.

His hand extends, a trembling, weathered plea—
The coins he cradles like a distant prayer,
Each piece is a memory, a history
Of days when youth was free, of moments rare.

The clink, the clink—the sound so small, so slight,
Yet in its echo, ghosts begin to rise.
Each coin a key, unlocking fading light,
A door to distant suns and clouded skies.

Once, in the village square, he danced and sang,
A young man, proud, with fire in his chest.
His pocket heavy with the joy it rang,
Coins spun and sparkled—life had been his guest.

The world was bright, as bright as morning sun,
With endless roads and dreams that stretched afar.
His fingers brushed the golden threads that spun.
A future carved beneath a star.

But coins, like time, are fickle, swift to fall—
The wind, a thief, who steals both youth and trust.
The laughter wanes, the joy a distant call,
And hearts grow heavy, turning into dust.

Now, sitting still, he watches others pass,
Their hurried steps were a blur of silent grace.
He clinks his coins and feels the weight of glass.
That once was filled with promise, now erased.

With every coin, a face begins to form—
A lover's smile, a mother's tender touch,

A brother's laugh, a warmth that kept him warm,
A friend who promised never to lose touch.

But promises are brittle, worn with time,
Like threads that fray beneath the pressure's weight.
And those he loved? Their faces turn to rhyme,
Familiar words, but words that cannot wait.

His hand holds steady as the coins slip free,
A quiet dance, a sound that cuts the air,
And in that clang, he feels a strange decree—
The past, it whispers, then is lost, somewhere.

Each coin, a chapter, fading into rust,
Each coin, a face, a name, a quiet song.
He thinks of them—the lovers, those he trusted,
The ones who left, the ones who did him wrong.

The years were harsh, like winter's bitter wind,
The warmth of those old days is now far away.
Yet in his palm, the past is still pinned,
A fleeting kiss from yesterday.

He wonders, now, if they remember him—
The friends, the faces, all that once was bright.
But answers come like shadows in the dim,
A fading spark, a flicker in the night.

The coins, they sing their song of joy and pain,
A lullaby that weaves through his refrain.
And as he rattles them in shaking hands,
He knows that life is never as it stands.

For though the world has left him on the street,
Though hunger gnaws and time has stripped him bare,
His coins still hold a rhythm, soft, complete—
A memory of who he was, once there.

Each coin is a link to days that used to glow,
Each coin is a sign that somewhere, long ago,

There was a man who loved, who laughed, who dreamed,
And in his heart, he still hears the echo, still beams.

The beggar sighs, and with a final clink,
He lets the coins fall gently through his palm,
And as they scatter on the earth, they sink.
Into the soil, a soft and quiet calm.

For though the world moves on and leaves him cold,
The past is never gone—it's always gold.

His fingers curl, and yet the coins remain,
Each one a shard of something he once had—
A life that glittered, briefly in the rain,
A fleeting moment in the days gone bad.

He hears the clang, the chime, a rhythmic pulse,
A steady heartbeat in his weathered chest.
And in those sounds, he feels the fleeting pulse.
Of all he lost, of all he tried to wrest.

A lifetime's worth of roads he could not take,
Of lovers' eyes he never once could trust,
Of promises that vanished like the lake,
Of dreams that, like the coins, had turned to dust.

The city moves, indifferent to his plea,
The hurried crowd, a rush of nameless faces.
They do not know the weight of what they see—
The story is told in worn-out shoes and traces.

His eyes, like windows cracked by years of rain,
Still hold the gleam of someone once alive,
A man who laughed, who danced, who felt the strain
Of all the love and joy that helped him thrive.

But now, the sky is dark and far away,
The sun a memory too distant, faint.
His body aches, his spirit starts to fray,
And yet the coins, they never lose their quaint.

They keep him tethered, though the world has moved.
Beyond the reach of all he used to know.
He traces every face, each life he loved,
A mournful thread ties him to the flow.

With every clink, another face returns—
A child he once held in his strong embrace,
A lover lost, the fire that once did burn,
The friend who promised they would share the space.

And yet—oh, yet—how time has robbed him blind,
How coins have slipped through fingers, gone astray,
How memories that once were clear and kind
Now lie in fragments, scattered far away.

Still, he holds on, a beggar by the gate,
His life is reduced to coins and fleeting dreams.
But in the quiet, he can almost wait,
And hear the past, as distant as it seems.

For though the world may turn, the years may fade,
There is a rhythm here that will not die.
The coins that speak of love, of loss, of trade,
Still echo soft beneath the endless sky.

He thinks of days when laughter filled the air,
When hopes were bright and coins had weight and worth.
Now silence reigns, the days are cold and bare—
Yet still, these coins remind him of his birth.

They carry with them ghosts of who he was,
A man who dared to dream, who dared to run,
A heart once filled with love, once full of cause,
Now lost beneath the city's setting sun.

But still—still—he clings to them, those tiny things,
Like anchors dropped in seas of fading light,
And though the world has lost its golden rings,
The coins remind him that he once had flight.

In every flicker of their tender clang,
He hears the whisper of a life well-spent—
The days when hope still wore a golden fang,
The years when love was all he'd ever meant.

And so, he sits and lets the coins slip through,
Each sound a prayer, each clink a memory.
Though he may never find the world he knew,
In every coin, he finds eternity.

For in this life, it's not the things we hold—
Not coins, not riches, not the fleeting days—
But moments, soft and fleeting, yet so bold,
That lingers like the songs we used to raise.

83/83

♡ .- --.. . . -- .-

I lost my voice calling for you, in my mind,

I am a poet still lost for words to put you into existence,

A pen and paper are just not enough to describe my love and fancy for you.

I'll whisper slowly into your ears with grace if you could make a promise to stay, a solid vow.

84/84

♡ .- --.. . . -- .- --..-- -- .. -. .

I'd be the shallow sea, you'd be the waves in it,
I own my heart, but you are its rhythm.
I want us to be forever,
But would we?
85/85

Dear Reader,

First of all, I want to extend my deepest gratitude to you for taking the time to read this book. In a world where distractions are endless and time is precious, the simple act of picking up a book, especially a poetry collection, is a gift. So, thank you for sharing your time, your attention, and your heart with my words. It is no small thing, and I am incredibly humbled that you have allowed me into your thoughts.

When I first set out to write these poems, I never imagined that they would find their way into your hands. The process of creating this book has been both a journey of self-discovery and an exploration of the human experience. I've written these poems as a way to untangle the messiness of my own thoughts, my own feelings. To capture the fleeting moments of joy and sorrow, beauty and pain, that make up the tapestry of life. And now, as you hold these words in your hands, I realize how deeply they belong not just to me but to you as well. After all, it is not just the voice of the writer—it is the heart of the reader, too.

The Journey of Writing

Writing poetry has always felt like both a sacred and a personal act, a way to bridge the gap between what I can articulate in the silence of my own mind and what can be shared with others. It is an intimate process, one that often makes us feel vulnerable. I write to make sense of the world, to give voice to the feelings and thoughts that are often too complex for ordinary language. And yet, as much as I write for myself, I write to connect with you—whoever you are, wherever you may be.

This book didn't come together overnight. It has been a collection of fragments, some penned in moments of intense emotion, others in quiet reflection. There are poems that came to me like lightning bolts, arriving fully formed in the span of a few minutes. There are others that took years to shape, their meaning elusive, their words elusive until they finally clicked into place. Poetry, I've found, is like that—sometimes a swift flood, other times a slow, careful chiseling.

But in every line, every stanza, I poured my heart. These poems are not perfect; they are raw, messy, and unfinished in many ways. But I think that's what makes them human, and that's why they matter. It is the imperfection of our existence that gives it meaning, and it is in the brokenness that we often find our most profound truths.

The Themes: Life, Love, Loss, and Memory

As you read these poems, you may have noticed certain recurring themes—life, love, loss, memory, identity, and the search for meaning. These are the threads that run through the tapestry of my experience, and I suspect they resonate with you, too. Because, in truth, these are universal themes. We all navigate the complexity of relationships, the depth of love, the pain of loss, and the constant questioning of who we are and what we want.

In some ways, this book is a reflection of the many lives I've lived—both the ones I've experienced firsthand and the ones I've witnessed in others. The love I've felt, the losses I've mourned, the fleeting beauty I've tried to hold onto. We are all shaped by our experiences, and the moments we live through—both the extraordinary and the mundane—become the stories that define us. I hope this book speaks to the parts of you that have been touched by similar experiences. Perhaps, when you read a poem, it reminds you of a moment from your own life, a feeling that you thought you had buried, or a thought you had long since forgotten.

Some of the poems are about joy—the quiet, everyday moments that are easy to overlook but are so precious. These are the moments when we are fully alive, when we are present in our own lives, and when we feel deeply connected to the world around us. But not all of the poems are about joy. Some of them explore the darker side of the human experience: the pain of loss, the isolation we sometimes feel, the confusion and sorrow that come with the passing of time. But even in these moments of sadness, there is beauty. I truly believe that even the most painful experiences can be transformed into something meaningful when we allow ourselves to face them, sit with them, and reflect on their lessons.

The Role of Memory and Reflection

One of the central themes that runs throughout this collection is memory—the way we hold onto fragments of our past, and how those fragments shape who we are today. Memory is a funny thing. It's a puzzle made up of pieces we try to fit together, but often, the pieces don't match. We remember things differently than how they happened. Sometimes, the past is clearer than the present, and sometimes, the present slips away faster than we can catch it.

I've often wondered about the role memory plays in the stories we tell ourselves. Do we remember things the way they truly were, or do we remember them the way we need them to be? Memory is both a lens and a filter—it shapes our reality, it filters our experiences, and it tells us who we were and who we are. But it's not always reliable. And that's okay. It's part of being human.

In my poems, I've tried to capture moments of remembering—those fleeting glimpses of the past that come rushing back when we least expect them. Sometimes, memory is a source of comfort, a reminder of the people we've loved, the places we've been, and the experiences that have shaped us. But other times, it is a heavy burden, a weight we carry with us, filled with regrets and unanswered questions. Yet, even in the shadow of these memories, there is beauty. There is growth. And there is always the potential for healing.

The Act of Reading

I believe that the act of reading poetry is an act of communion. When you read these words, you are connected in some way, even if only for a brief moment. You are no longer just a passive consumer of these poems—you become an active participant in the experience. Poetry, I think, lives not just in the words written on the page but in the space between the lines, in the way the reader interprets them. It is a conversation between the writer and the reader, even when no words are spoken.

When you read poetry, you engage with it on a deeper level. You bring your own experiences, your own interpretations, and your own feelings to the work. That is what makes poetry so powerful. It transcends the individual; it becomes a collective experience. The emotions that I have poured into these poems are now intertwined with yours, and together, we've created something new. This book is as much yours as it is mine.

The Power of Poetry

Poetry has a special power to speak to the soul in a way that other forms of writing sometimes cannot. It is more than just language—it is music, rhythm, and emotion all wrapped into one. It distills experience into its purest form, capturing the essence of a feeling, a moment, or an idea. And though poetry may be brief, it is never shallow. In its brevity, it has the ability to evoke entire worlds.

When I write, I think about the way words can touch the heart, the way a single line can shift someone's perspective, the way a poem can bring clarity to confusion, or comfort to sorrow. Poetry is a mirror, reflecting the world as it is, but also as it could be. It reminds us of the things we often overlook, the beauty hidden in the everyday, and the depth that exists in the smallest of moments.

It is my hope that in reading this book, you have found something that resonates with you—that a line or a stanza spoke to your heart or that you recognized a part of yourself in these words. That is the magic of poetry: it creates a space where the personal becomes universal, where our shared experiences of joy, sorrow, love, and loss connect us in profound ways.

A Final Thank You

As you close this book, I want you to know how deeply grateful I am for you. You, the reader, are the final piece in the puzzle of this collection. Without you, these poems would simply be words on a page, but with you, they have found their true purpose. Your reading, your interpretation, and your engagement with these poems breathe life into them.

So, thank you once again for your time, for your heart, and for your willingness to share in this journey with me. My hope is that, as you turn the last page and step back into your world, something from these poems stays with you. A thought. A feeling. A question. A memory. Because if I've managed to stir something inside you, then this book has fulfilled its purpose. And that, to me, is everything.

With deepest gratitude,
Kaachu